How Animals Smell, Taste and Touch

Written by Jo Winds...

T0351216

Finding out about the world

Like humans, most animals can smell, taste and touch. These **senses** help animals to find out about the world around them.

Mosquitoes are brilliant at sniffing out people. They really like the smell of sweaty feet!

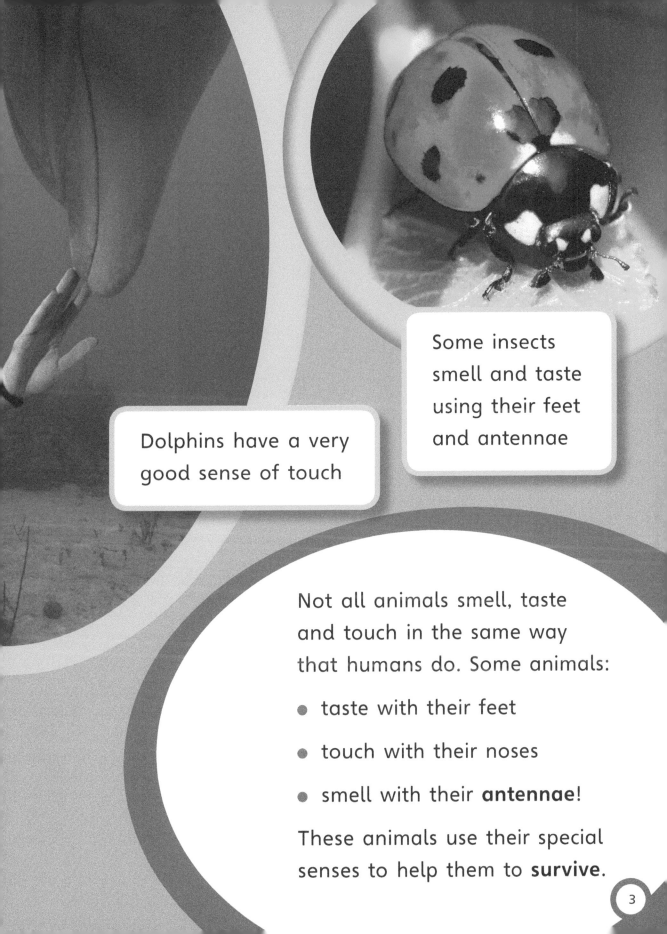

Dolphins have a very good sense of touch

Some insects smell and taste using their feet and antennae

Not all animals smell, taste and touch in the same way that humans do. Some animals:

- taste with their feet

- touch with their noses

- smell with their **antennae**!

These animals use their special senses to help them to **survive**.

Super smell

Some animals have a super sense of smell. This is useful in many ways. It can help animals to **detect** danger. It can help them to sniff out food, or find a **mate**.

Smelling the air even helps some animals to find water in dry places. Elephants have an excellent sense of smell. They can smell water from five kilometres away.

nostrils

Elephants raise their trunks to sniff the air

Polar bears are champion smellers

Bears use their super sense of smell to find food. Polar bears can smell food, such as seals, under the ice.

Emperor moths

The world's sharpest sense of smell belongs to an animal without a nose! Emperor moths smell using their large antennae.

Air flows over the antennae as the moths move. The antennae are covered in smelling **receptors**, which pick up smells in the air.

Emperor moths use their amazing sense of smell to find other moths. Male moths can smell female moths from as far as 11 kilometres away.

eye

antennae

head

A close-up picture of a moth's feathery antennae

A male Emperor moth

Shark snacks

Sharks have a better sense of smell than any other fish. They can sniff out a tiny drop of blood from one kilometre away! This helps them to find food in huge oceans.

snout

Sharks smell using two special places under their **snouts**. This is a great white shark

Hammerhead sharks' strange heads may help them to work out where a smell is coming from

Great white sharks love to eat seals and sea lions. Scientists think these sharks stick their heads out of the water to sniff out their favourite food.

Nose to the ground

Many animals have a much better sense of smell than humans do. We have about five million smell receptors in our noses. This is enough to smell 10,000 different smells.

This mountain rescue dog is looking for people trapped under the snow

Dogs can be trained to sniff out truffles, a type of mushroom that grows underground

Dogs have around 200 million smell receptors! Police and rescue dogs can be trained to sniff out anything the police want to find, such as:

- trapped or missing people
- people who have carried out a crime
- dangerous poisons
- hidden objects.

Top taste

Humans taste things by using our tongues. These are covered in **taste buds**, which help us to work out if something is good to eat.

An earthworm is like a long, wriggly tongue! Its body is covered in taste buds

tentacle

sucker

Octopuses taste things by using the suckers on their **tentacles**

Some animals can taste an object without putting it into their mouth! A special sense of taste using other parts of their bodies helps these animals to find food or mates.

Snakes and lizards

Not all tongues can taste! A snake's tongue has no taste buds. It is only used to bring tastes into the snake's mouth.

As the snake's tongue flicks out, it collects tiny bits of material from the air and ground. Then the tongue flicks back inside the snake's mouth. There is a special area on the roof of the snake's mouth. This tastes everything on the snake's tongue. The snake can work out if there is **prey** nearby.

A snake can taste things without touching them

Some lizards taste the air in the same way as snakes do. They use their special skill to find a mate

Fins and barbels

Fish can have taste buds almost anywhere on their bodies. Some fish have taste buds on their fins. They can taste food just by brushing against it.

A catfish's barbels are covered in taste buds

barbel

fin

Searobins have taste buds at the tips of their fins. They can taste food just by touching it

Some fish have taste buds all over their bodies. Catfish are covered in more than 100,000 taste buds. This is ten times more than humans have!

Catfish also have special body parts growing from their heads. They look like whiskers, but they are called **barbels**. Catfish can taste food with their barbels.

Insects

Some insects have taste buds shaped like tiny hairs. Each hair can tell the different tastes of sugar, water and salt.

The hairs are usually found near an insect's mouth. Some insects have taste buds on other parts of their body, such as their feet! This is handy for insects that land on food feet-first.

Flies use their mouths and feet to taste the things they land on

Some flies have up to 3,000 taste buds on their feet

A butterfly rolls its proboscis into a tasty flower

tasting hair

mouth

proboscis

Butterflies taste with their feet. When a butterfly finds out it is standing on something yummy, it rolls down its long **proboscis** to suck up the food.

Terrific touch

For humans to feel something, we usually have to be close enough to touch it. Some animals have a super sense of touch. They can feel the world around them without touching anything. They can even feel things that are far away.

Sea anemones look like flowers. They are really animals with an amazing sense of touch!

Sea anemones use their sense of touch to catch food. When a fish brushes against one of the anemone's tentacles, it **triggers** a poisonous sting.

Seals use their whiskers to feel fish from a distance, and work out which are best to eat

Whiskers help cats to feel exactly how far away they are from objects around them

Elephants

Hold your hand flat on a table as somebody knocks on the surface. Can you feel the **vibrations**? Some animals have special body parts to help them sense vibrations.

Amazing touch means elephants can **communicate** by stamping

Elephants stamp the ground with their feet when they feel **alarmed**. They are not trying to look scary. They are warning other elephants about danger.

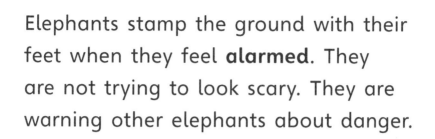

An elephant's foot has special touch sensors in the sole

sole

Vibrations from the stamping travel through the ground. Other elephants pick up the vibrations through their feet. They can feel vibrations from a stamping elephant up to 50 kilometres away!

Fish

Fish can feel vibrations in the water. They have a special groove that runs along their body and onto their head. There are sense receptors inside the groove. These sense tiny movements in the water.

Feeling from a distance helps fish to swim close together without bumping into each other

As a fish swims, it makes ripples in the water. The ripples travel away from the fish and bounce off anything around it. The ripples bounce back towards the fish. The fish feels the moving water. Its super sense of touch tells it what is nearby.

sense receptors

A special line along the side of their bodies helps fish to feel things from a distance

Bugs and spiders

Bugs are brilliant at feeling vibrations. Cockroaches can sense air movements as tiny as the breeze from a wasp's wings. When a cockroach feels the air moving, it runs. Nothing can sneak up on it.

Cockroaches are the world's best animals at feeling vibrations

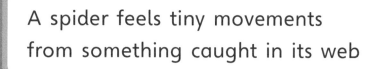

A spider feels tiny movements from something caught in its web

Most spiders can't see very well. They use their sense of touch to find food. Some spiders have special hairs on their legs to sense vibrations. They can feel vibrations from the wings of an insect that is flying towards them.

Star-nosed mole

Star-nosed moles live in dark underground tunnels. They aren't very good at seeing or hearing. But their amazing sense of touch helps them to find food.

A star-nosed mole about to go hunting

As a star-nosed mole crawls along, the tentacles on its snout touch everything around it. The mole can feel 12 things every second and work out what they are! It gobbles up anything that feels delicious, such as worms and insects.

Star-nosed moles have 22 touchy-feely tentacles on their snouts

tentacle

Quiz

(1) What do Emperor moths use to smell?

   a feet

   b antennae

   c nose

(2) What are police sniffer dogs trained to look for?

   a missing truffles

   b missing people

   c missing dog food

(3) Which animal can taste food without touching it?

   a snake

   b butterfly

   c earthworm

(4) Where are a fish's special touch receptors found?

   a on its tail

   b on the top of its body

   c on the side of its body

Answers on page 31

Glossary

alarmed	feels in danger
antennae	pair of body parts on an insect's head
barbels	finger-like body parts growing from a fish's head
communicate	share information
detect	discover or find something
mate	one of a pair that breed (have babies) together
prey	animal that is hunted for food
proboscis	butterfly's tube-like tongue
receptors	tiny body parts that can sense something, such as smell or taste
senses	used by an animal to find out about the world around it
snout	nose and mouth that stick out from the rest of an animal's head
survive	stay alive
taste buds	tiny body parts for sensing taste
tentacle	bendy body part used to grab or touch things
triggers	sets off
vibrations	tiny shaking movements

Quiz answers: 1b; 2b; 3a; 4c

Index

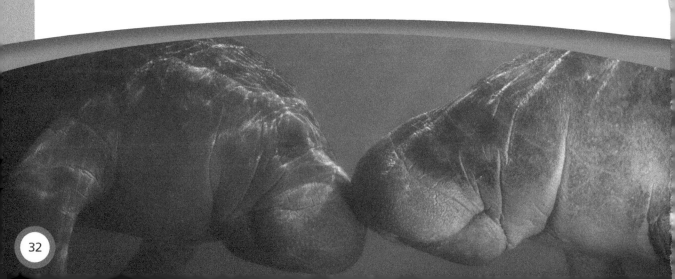